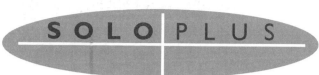

Alto Saxophone

Cover photography by Randall Wallace
Arranged and performed by David Pearl

Order No. AM 947452
US International Standard Book Number: 0.8256.1682.4
UK International Standard Book Number: 0.7119.6953.1

Exclusive Distributors:
Music Sales Corporation
257 Park Avenue South, New York, NY 10010 USA
Music Sales Limited
8/9 Frith Street, London W1V 5TZ England
Music Sales Pty. Limited
120 Rothschild Street, Rosebery, Sydney, NSW 2018, Australia

Printed in the United States of America by
Vicks Lithograph and Printing Corporation

Amsco Publications
New York/London/Sydney

Contents

A Frangesa

Costa

A Media Luz

E. Donato

Allemande

Franz Joseph Haydn

Amaryllis

H. Ghys

Arirang

Korean Folk Song

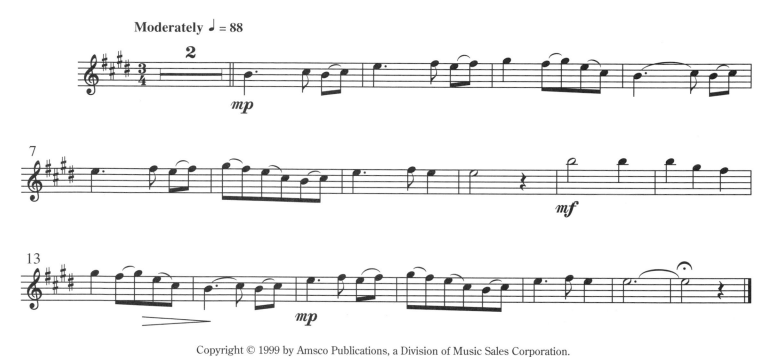

The Beautiful Jasmine

Ancient Chinese Melody

Bourée

Leopold Mozart

El Coqui

Puerto Rican Folk Song

Dubula

Shoot

African Folk Song

Grand March
from *Aida*

Giuseppe Verdi

The Cowherd's Song

Edvard Grieg

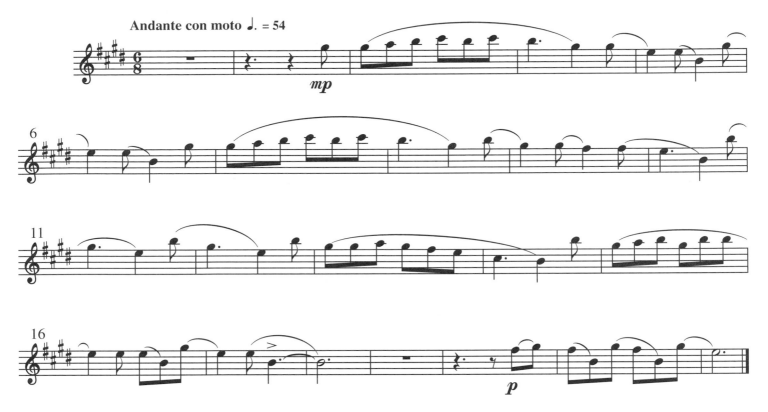

The Happy Farmer

Robert Schumann

Matilda

Jamaican Folk Song

Moderately slow calypso ♩= 69

Merry Widow Waltz

Franz Lehár

Harmony Rag

Hal Nichols

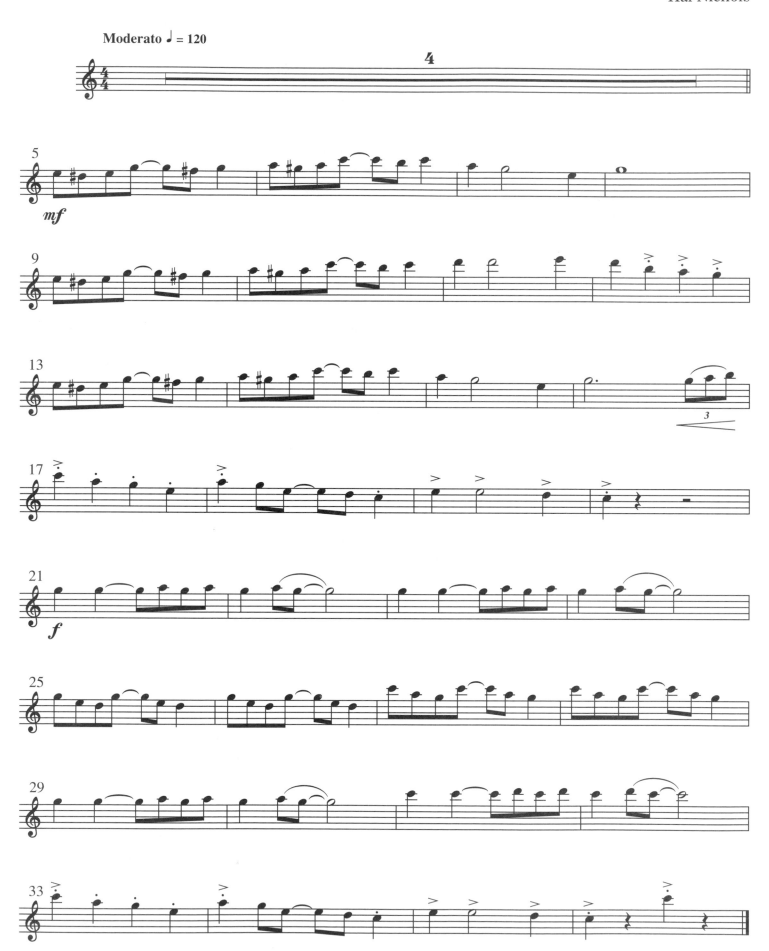

Plaisir d'Amour

Giovanni Martini

Minuet
from *Violin Concerto K. 219*

Wolfgang Amadeus Mozart

14

Rondo Aragonesa

Allegro ♩ = 138

Enrique Granados

Slovakian Dance Tune

Traditional

Lively ♩ = 104

Song of Kokkiriko

Japanese Folk Song

Solace

Scott Joplin

Song of the North

Edvard Grieg

Trio

Johann Sebastian Bach

The Happy Farmer

Robert Schumann

Matilda

Jamaican Folk Song

Moderately slow calypso ♩ = 69

Merry Widow Waltz

Franz Lehár

Harmony Rag

Hal Nichols

Moderato ♩ = 120

Plaisir d'Amour

Giovanni Martini

Minuet
from *Violin Concerto K. 219*

Wolfgang Amadeus Mozart

Tempo di minuetto ♩ = 88

Rondo Aragonesa

Enrique Granados

Slovakian Dance Tune

Traditional

Song of Kokkiriko

Japanese Folk Song

Solace

Very slow march

Scott Joplin

Song of the North

Edvard Grieg

Trio

Johann Sebastian Bach